MW01491315

THE ORDER OF BAPTISM OF CHILDREN

ENGLISH TRANSLATION ACCORDING TO THE SECOND TYPICAL EDITION

For Use in the Dioceses of the United States of America

Approved by the
United States Conference of Catholic Bishops
and Confirmed by the Apostolic See

2020

LITURGICAL PRESS
Collegeville, Minnesota

www.litpress.org

Nihil Obstat: Reverend Robert Harren, J.C.L., *Censor deputatus*.

Imprimatur: ✛ Most Reverend Donald J. Kettler, J.C.L., Bishop of Saint Cloud, October 29, 2019.

Published with the approval of the Committee on Divine Worship, United States Conference of Catholic Bishops.

Cover design by Monica Bokinskie. Art by Frank Kacmarcik, OblSB.

Published by Liturgical Press, Collegeville, Minnesota. Printed in the United States of America.

ISBN 978-0-8146-6578-7

CHRISTIAN INITIATION

Through the Sacraments of Christian Initiation all who have been freed from the power of darkness and have died, been buried and been raised with Christ, receive the Spirit of filial adoption and celebrate with the entire People of God the memorial of the Lord's Death and Resurrection.[1]

For, having been incorporated into Christ through Baptism, they are formed into the People of God, and, having received the remission of all their sins and been rescued from the power of darkness, they are brought to the status of adopted sons and daughters,[2] being made a new creation by water and the Holy Spirit. Hence they are called, and indeed are, children of God.[3] Sealed with the gift of the same Spirit in Confirmation, they are more perfectly configured to the Lord and filled with the Holy Spirit, so that bearing witness to Christ before the world, they bring the Body of Christ to its full stature without delay.[4] Finally, participating in the Eucharistic assembly (*synaxis*), they eat the Flesh and drink the Blood of the Son of Man, so that they may receive eternal life[5] and show forth the unity of God's people. Offering themselves with Christ, they take part in the universal sacrifice, which is

---

1. Second Vatican Council, Decree on the Church's Missionary Activity, *Ad gentes*, no. 14.
2. Cf. Colossians 1:13; Romans 8:15; Galatians 4:5. Cf. also Council of Trent, sess. 6., *Decr. de justificatione*, cap. 4: Denz.-Schön. 1524.
3. Cf. 1 John 3:1.
4. Cf. Second Vatican Council, Decree on the Church's Missionary Activity, *Ad gentes*, no. 36.
5. Cf. John 6:55.

the entire city of the redeemed offered to God through the great High Priest;[6] they also pray that, through a fuller outpouring of the Holy Spirit, the whole human race come into the unity of God's family.[7] Thus the three Sacraments of Christian Initiation so work together that they bring to full stature the Christian faithful, who exercise in the Church and in the world the mission of the entire Christian people.[8]

Baptism, the door to life and to the Kingdom, is the first Sacrament of the New Law, which Christ offered to all that they might have eternal life[9] and which, together with the Gospel, he later entrusted to his Church, when he commanded his Apostles: "Go, teach all nations, baptizing them in the name of the Father, and of the Son, and of the Holy Spirit."[10] Therefore Baptism is first and foremost the Sacrament of that faith by which human beings, enlightened by the grace of the Holy Spirit, respond to the Gospel of Christ. That is why the Church believes that there is nothing more ancient and nothing more proper for herself than to urge all—catechumens, parents of children who are to be baptized, and godparents—to that true and active faith by which, as they hold fast to Christ, they enter into or confirm the New Covenant. In fact, the pastoral instruction of catechumens and the preparation of parents, as well as the celebration of God's Word and the profession of baptismal faith, are all ordered to this end.

Furthermore, Baptism is the Sacrament by which human beings are incorporated into the Church and are built up together into a dwelling place of God in the Spirit,[11] and into a royal priesthood and a holy nation;[12] it is also a sacramental bond of unity linking all who are

---

6. Cf. Saint Augustine, *De civitate Dei* 10, 6: PL 41, 284. Vatican Council II, Dogmatic Constitution on the Church, *Lumen gentium*, no. 11; Decree on the Ministry and Life of Priests, *Presbyterorum ordinis*, no. 2.
7. Cf. Second Vatican Council, Dogmatic Constitution on the Church, *Lumen gentium*, no. 28.
8. Cf. *ibidem*, no. 31.
9. Cf. John 3:5.
10. Matthew 28:19.
11. Cf. Ephesians 2:22.
12. Cf. 1 Peter 2:9.

signed by it.[13] Because of that unchangeable effect (which the very celebration of the Sacrament in the Latin Liturgy makes clear when the baptized are anointed with Chrism, in the presence of the People of God), the rite of Baptism is held in highest honor by all Christians. Nor is it lawful for anyone to repeat it once it has been validly celebrated, even by separated brethren.

Moreover, the washing with water in the word of life,[14] which is what Baptism is, cleanses human beings of every stain of sin, both original and personal, and makes them sharers in the divine nature[15] and in filial adoption.[16] For Baptism, as is proclaimed in the prayers for the blessing of water, is the washing of regeneration[17] of the children of God and of birth from on high. The invocation of the Most Holy Trinity over those who are to be baptized has the effect that, signed with this name, they are consecrated to the Trinity and enter into fellowship with the Father, and the Son, and the Holy Spirit. This is the high point for which the biblical readings, the prayer of the community, and the threefold profession of faith prepare, and to which they lead.

Baptism, far superior to the purifications of the Old Law, produces these effects by virtue of the mystery of the Lord's Passion and Resurrection. Those who are baptized are united with Christ in a death like his, are buried with him in death,[18] and also in him are given life and are raised up.[19] For in Baptism nothing other than the Paschal Mystery is recalled and accomplished, because in it human beings pass from the death of sin into life. Therefore, the joy of the resurrection should shine forth in the celebration of Baptism, especially when it takes place during the Easter Vigil or on a Sunday.

---

13. Cf. Second Vatican Council, Decree on Ecumenism, *Unitatis redintegratio*, no. 22.
14. Cf. Ephesians 5:26.
15. Cf. 2 Peter 1:4.
16. Cf. Romans 8:15; Galatians 4:5.
17. Cf. Titus 3:5.
18. Cf. Romans 6:5, 4.
19. Cf. Ephesians 2:5-6.

ORDER OF BAPTISM
FOR SEVERAL CHILDREN

Rite of Receiving the Children

Baptism should be celebrated, insofar as possible, on a Sunday, the day on which the Church recalls the Paschal Mystery, and indeed in a common celebration for all the newly born, and with the attendance of a large number of the faithful, or at least of the relatives, friends, and neighbors, and with their active participation.

It is for the father and mother, together with the godparents, to present the child to the Church for Baptism.

If there are very many children to be baptized, and there are several Priests or Deacons present, these may assist the celebrant in performing those rites that are indicated in the text.

The faithful sing a suitable Psalm or hymn, if circumstances allow. Meanwhile, the Priest or Deacon celebrant, wearing an alb or surplice and stole, and even a cope, in a festive color, goes with the ministers to the door of the church, or to that part of the church where the parents and godparents are gathered with those to be baptized.

The celebrant greets those present, especially the parents and godparents, recalling in a few words the joy with which the parents received their children as a gift from God, who is the source of all life and who now wishes to bestow his own life on them. He may use these or similar words:

Dear parents and godparents:
Your families have experienced great joy at the birth of your children,
and the Church shares your happiness.
Today this joy has brought you to the Church
to give thanks to God for the gift of your children
and to celebrate a new birth in the waters of Baptism.
This community rejoices with you,
for today the number of those baptized in Christ will be increased,
and we offer you our support in raising your children
in the practice of the faith.
Therefore, brothers and sisters,
let us now prepare ourselves to participate in this celebration,
listening to God's Word, praying for these children and their families,
and renewing our commitment to the Lord and to his people.

The celebrant first asks the parents of each child:

What name do you give (or: have you given) your child?

Parents:

N.

Celebrant:

What do you ask of God's Church for N.?

Parents:

Baptism.

The celebrant may use other words in this dialogue.

The first reply may be given by another person if, according to local custom, this person has the right to give the name.

In the second reply, the parents may use other words: e.g., Faith or The grace of Christ or Entry into the Church or Eternal life.

If there are many to be baptized, the celebrant may ask all the parents at once for the names of their children:

What name do you give (or: have you given) your child?

Each family replies in turn. The second question may be put to all at once in the plural.

Celebrant:
What do you ask of God's Church for your children?

All:
Baptism.

Then the celebrant addresses the parents in these or similar words:
In asking for Baptism for your children,
you are undertaking the responsibility
of raising them in the faith,
so that, keeping God's commandments,
they may love the Lord and their neighbor as Christ has taught us.
Do you understand this responsibility?

Parents:
We do.

This reply is given by each family individually; but if the number of children to be baptized is very large, the reply may be given by all together.

Then turning to the godparents, the celebrant asks in these or similar words:
Are you ready to help the parents of these children in their duty?

All the godparents together:
We are.

Then the celebrant continues, saying:
N. and N. (or: Dear children),
the Church of God receives you with great joy.
In her name I sign you with the Sign of the Cross of Christ our Savior;
then, after me, your parents (and godparents) will do the same.

And, without saying anything, he signs each of the children on the forehead. Afterwards he invites the parents, and if it seems appropriate, the godparents, to do the same.

The celebrant invites the parents, godparents, and others present to take part in the celebration of the Word of God. If circumstances permit, a procession to the appointed place takes place with singing (e.g., Psalm 85 [84]:7-9ab).

PSALM 85 (84):7-9AB

Will you not restore again our life,
   that your people may rejoice in you?
Show us, O LORD, your mercy,
   and grant us your salvation.
I will hear what the LORD God speaks;
   he speaks of peace for his people and his faithful.

The children to be baptized may be taken to a separate place, until the celebration of the Word of God is completed.

Sacred Celebration of the Word of God

BIBLICAL READINGS AND HOMILY

If it seems appropriate, one, or even two, of the following passages is read, while all are seated.

Mt 28:18-20: *Go, therefore, and make disciples of all nations, baptizing them in the name of the Father, and of the Son, and of the Holy Spirit* (p. 50).

Mk 1:9-11: *Jesus was baptized in the Jordan by John* (p. 50).

Mk 10:13-16: *Let the children come to me; do not prevent them* (p. 51).

Jn 3:1-6: *No one can see the Kingdom of God without being born from above* (p. 52).

The passages that are to be found on pp. 41–46 and 50–56, or others suited to the wishes or needs of the parents, may also be chosen.

Between the Readings, the Responsorial Psalms or the Verses provided on pp. 46–49 may be sung.

After the Reading, the celebrant preaches a brief homily in which light is shed on what has been read, and those present are led to a deeper understanding of the mystery of Baptism and to a more eager fulfillment of the responsibility that arises from it, especially for parents and godparents.

After the Homily, or after the Litany, or even during the Litany, it is recommended that there be a period of silence in which all, invited by the celebrant, pray in their hearts.

PRAYER OF THE FAITHFUL

Then the Prayer of the Faithful takes place.

Celebrant:

Dear brothers and sisters,
let us invoke the mercy of our Lord Jesus Christ
for these children about to receive the grace of Baptism,
and for their parents, godparents, and all the baptized.

Lector:

Give these children new birth in Baptism
through the radiant divine mystery of your Death and Resurrection,
and join them to your holy Church:

All:

Lord, we ask you, hear our prayer.

Lector:

Make them faithful disciples and witnesses to your Gospel
through Baptism and Confirmation:

All:

Lord, we ask you, hear our prayer.

Lector:

Lead them through holiness of life
to the joys of the heavenly Kingdom:

All:

Lord, we ask you, hear our prayer.

Lector:

Make their parents and godparents
a shining example of the faith to these children:

All:

Lord, we ask you, hear our prayer.

Keep their families always in your love:

Lord, we ask you, hear our prayer.

Lector:
Renew the grace of Baptism in each of us:

All:
Lord, we ask you, hear our prayer.

Other optional formulas may be used.

Afterwards, the celebrant invites those present to invoke the aid of the Saints (if the circumstances require, the children are brought back into the church):

Holy Mary, Mother of God,	**pray for us.**
Saint John the Baptist,	**pray for us.**
Saint Joseph,	**pray for us.**
Saint Peter and Saint Paul,	**pray for us.**

It is good to add the names of other Saints, especially those who are Patron Saints of the children or of the church or of the place. Then the Litany concludes:

All holy men and women, Saints of God,	**pray for us.**

Optional extended form of the Litany may be used.

PRAYER OF EXORCISM AND ANOINTING BEFORE BAPTISM

After the invocations, the celebrant says:
Almighty ever-living God,
who sent your Son into the world
to drive out from us the power of Satan, the spirit of evil,
and bring the human race, rescued from darkness,
into the marvelous Kingdom of your light:
we humbly beseech you
to free these children from Original Sin,
to make them the temple of your glory,
and to grant that your Holy Spirit may dwell in them.
Through Christ our Lord.

Amen.

The celebrant continues:
May the strength of Christ the Savior protect you.
As a sign of this we anoint you with the oil of salvation
in the same Christ our Lord,
who lives and reigns for ever and ever.

All:
Amen.

Those to be baptized are anointed one at a time on the breast with the Oil of Catechumens. If there are many children, it is permitted to make use of several ministers.

In the United States, if, for serious reasons, the celebrant judges it pastorally necessary or desirable, the Anointing before Baptism may be omitted. In that case, the celebrant says only once:
May the strength of Christ the Savior protect you;
who lives and reigns for ever and ever.

All:
Amen.

And immediately, without saying anything, he lays his hand on each of the children.

Then, if the baptistery is outside the church or out of sight of the faithful, there is a procession to it.

But if it is located within view of the congregation, the celebrant, parents, and godparents go there with the children and the others remain in their places.

If the baptistery cannot accommodate all those present, it is permitted to celebrate the Baptism in a more suitable place, with the parents and godparents coming forward at the appropriate time.

Meanwhile, if it can be done with dignity, a suitable liturgical song is sung, e.g., Psalm 23 (22).

The Lord is my shepherd;
   there is nothing I shall want.
Fresh and green are the pastures
   where he gives me repose.
Near restful waters he leads me;
   he revives my soul.

He guides me along the right path,
   for the sake of his name.
Though I should walk in the valley of the shadow of death,
   no evil would I fear, for you are with me.
Your crook and your staff will give me comfort.

You have prepared a table before me
   in the sight of my foes.
My head you have anointed with oil;
   my cup is overflowing.

Surely goodness and mercy shall follow me
   all the days of my life.
In the Lord's own house shall I dwell
   for length of days unending.

Celebration of Baptism

When they have come to the font, the celebrant briefly reminds those present of the wonderful plan of God, who willed to sanctify the human soul and body through water. He may do this in these or similar words:

A Let us pray, dear brothers and sisters,
   that the Lord God Almighty may bestow new life on these children
   by water and the Holy Spirit.

14

Or:

B Dear brothers and sisters,
you know that God graciously bestows
his abundant life through the sacrament of water
on those who believe.

Let us then raise our minds to him,
and with one heart pray
that he may be pleased to pour out his grace from this font
upon these chosen ones.

BLESSING OF WATER AND INVOCATION OF GOD OVER THE WATER

Then, turning to the font, the celebrant says the following Blessing
(outside Easter Time):

O God, who by invisible power
accomplish a wondrous effect
through sacramental signs
and who in many ways have prepared water, your creation,
to show forth the grace of Baptism;

O God, whose Spirit
in the first moments of the world's creation
hovered over the waters,
so that the very substance of water
would even then take to itself the power to sanctify;

O God, who by the outpouring of the flood
foreshadowed regeneration,
so that from the mystery of one and the same element of water
would come an end to vice and a beginning of virtue;

O God, who caused the children of Abraham
to pass dry-shod through the Red Sea,
so that the chosen people,
set free from slavery to Pharaoh,
would prefigure the people of the baptized;

15

O God, whose Son,
baptized by John in the waters of the Jordan,
was anointed with the Holy Spirit,
and, as he hung upon the Cross,
gave forth water from his side along with blood,
and after his Resurrection, commanded his disciples:
"Go forth, teach all nations, baptizing them
in the name of the Father and of the Son and of the Holy Spirit,"
look now, we pray, upon the face of your Church
and graciously unseal for her the fountain of Baptism.

May this water receive by the Holy Spirit
the grace of your Only Begotten Son,
so that human nature, created in your image
and washed clean through the Sacrament of Baptism
from all the squalor of the life of old,
may be found worthy to rise to the life of newborn children
through water and the Holy Spirit.

The celebrant touches the water with his right hand and continues:
May the power of the Holy Spirit,
O Lord, we pray,
come down through your Son
into the fullness of this font,
so that all who have been buried with Christ
by Baptism into death
may rise again to life with him.
Who lives and reigns for ever and ever.

All:
Amen.

Other optional formulas may be used.

During Easter Time, however, if the baptismal water has been consecrated at the Easter Vigil, so that the Baptism may not lack the element of thanksgiving and petition, the blessing and invocation of God over the water takes place in accordance with the formulas found in the Order of Baptism, *using the textual variation given at the end of these same formulas.*

16

Renunciation of Sin and Profession of Faith

The celebrant instructs the parents and godparents in these words:
Dear parents and godparents:
through the Sacrament of Baptism
the children you have presented
are about to receive from the love of God
new life by water and the Holy Spirit.

For your part, you must strive to bring them up in the faith,
so that this divine life may be preserved from the contagion of sin,
and may grow in them day by day.

If your faith makes you ready to accept this responsibility,
then, mindful of your own Baptism,
renounce sin and profess faith in Christ Jesus,
the faith of the Church,
in which children are baptized.

Then the celebrant questions them:

A Do you renounce Satan?

Parents and godparents:
I do.

Celebrant:
And all his works?

Parents and godparents:
I do.

Celebrant:
And all his empty show?

Parents and godparents:
I do.

Or:

B Celebrant:

Do you renounce sin,
so as to live in the freedom of the children of God?

Parents and godparents:
I do.

Celebrant:

Do you renounce the lure of evil,
so that sin may have no mastery over you?

Parents and godparents:
I do.

Celebrant:

Do you renounce Satan,
the author and prince of sin?

Parents and godparents:
I do.

In the United States, if the occasion requires, this second formula may be adapted with more precision by the Diocesan Bishop, especially when it is necessary that the parents and godparents should renounce superstitions, divinations, and magical arts practiced with reference to the children.

Next, the celebrant elicits the threefold profession of faith by the parents and godparents, saying:

Do you believe in God,
the Father almighty,
Creator of heaven and earth?

Parents and godparents:
I do.

Celebrant:

Do you believe in Jesus Christ, his only Son, our Lord,
who was born of the Virgin Mary,
suffered death and was buried,
rose again from the dead
and is seated at the right hand of the Father?

Parents and godparents:
I do.

Celebrant:

Do you believe in the Holy Spirit,
the holy catholic Church,
the communion of saints,
the forgiveness of sins,
the resurrection of the body,
and life everlasting?

Parents and godparents:

I do.

The celebrant, together with the community, gives assent to this profession of faith, saying:

This is our faith. This is the faith of the Church.
We are proud to profess it in Christ Jesus our Lord.

All:

Amen.

Another formula may be substituted, if circumstances suggest. Or a suitable liturgical song, by which the community expresses its faith with one voice, may be sung.

BAPTISM

The celebrant invites the first family to approach the font. In addition, using the name of the individual child, he asks the parents and godparents:

Is it your will, therefore, that N. should receive Baptism in the faith of the Church, which we have all professed with you?

Parents and godparents:

It is.

And immediately the celebrant baptizes the child, saying:

N., I BAPTIZE YOU IN THE NAME OF THE FATHER,

He immerses the child or pours water over him (her) a first time.

AND OF THE SON,

He immerses the child or pours water over him (her) a second time.

AND OF THE HOLY SPIRIT.

He immerses the child or pours water over him (her) a third time.

He asks the same question and does the same for each child to be baptized.

After the Baptism of each child, it is appropriate for the people to sing a short acclamation, such as:

Blessed be God, who chose you in Christ.

Other optional acclamations may be used.

If the Baptism is celebrated by the pouring of water, it is preferable for the child to be held by the mother (or by the father); however, where it is felt that the existing custom should be retained, the child may be held by the godmother (or by the godfather). If the Baptism is by immersion, the child is lifted from the sacred font by the same person.

If there are many children to be baptized, and there are several Priests or Deacons present, each of them may baptize some of the children, by using the same method and formula described above.

Explanatory Rites

ANOINTING AFTER BAPTISM

Then the celebrant says:

Almighty God, the Father of our Lord Jesus Christ,
has freed you from sin,
given you new birth by water and the Holy Spirit,
and joined you to his people.
He now anoints you with the Chrism of salvation,
so that you may remain members of Christ, Priest, Prophet and King,
unto eternal life.

All:

Amen.

Then, without saying anything, the celebrant anoints each baptized child with sacred Chrism on the crown of his (her) head.

If there are a large number of baptized children and there are several Priests or Deacons present, each of them may anoint some of the children with Chrism.

CLOTHING WITH A WHITE GARMENT

The celebrant says:
(N. and N.,) you have become a new creation
and have clothed yourselves in Christ.
May this white garment be a sign to you of your Christian dignity.
With your family and friends to help you by word and example,
bring it unstained into eternal life.

All:
Amen.

And a white garment is placed on each child; another color is not
permitted, unless it is demanded by local custom. It is desirable that the
families themselves provide this garment.

HANDING ON OF A LIGHTED CANDLE

The celebrant then takes the paschal candle and says:
Receive the light of Christ.

One member of each family (e.g., the father or godfather) lights a candle
for each child from the paschal candle.

Then the celebrant says:
Parents and godparents,
this light is entrusted to you to be kept burning brightly,
so that your children, enlightened by Christ,
may walk always as children of the light
and, persevering in the faith,
may run to meet the Lord when he comes
with all the Saints in the heavenly court.

"Ephphatha"

In the United States, the "Ephphatha" Rite takes place at the discretion of the celebrant. The celebrant touches the ears and mouth of each child with his thumb, saying:

May the Lord Jesus,
who made the deaf to hear and the mute to speak,
grant that you may soon receive his word with your ears
and profess the faith with your lips,
to the glory and praise of God the Father.

All:
Amen.

If there are many children, the celebrant says the formula once, omitting the touching of the ears and mouth.

Conclusion of the Rite

Afterwards, unless the Baptism took place in the sanctuary, there is a procession to the altar, in which the lighted candles of the newly baptized are carried.

Meanwhile, it is desirable that a baptismal canticle be sung, e.g.:
Baptized in Christ,
you are clothed with Christ,
alleluia, alleluia.

Lord's Prayer

The celebrant, standing before the altar, addresses the parents and godparents and all present in these or similar words:

Dear brothers and sisters:
these children, reborn through Baptism,
are now called children of God, for so indeed they are.

Through Confirmation they will receive the fullness of the Holy Spirit
and, approaching the altar of the Lord,
they will share at the table of his Sacrifice,

and will call upon God as Father in the midst of the Church.
Now in their name,
and in the spirit of adoption as sons and daughters
which we have all received,
let us pray together as the Lord taught us.

And all say together with the celebrant:
Our Father, who art in heaven,
hallowed be thy name;
thy kingdom come,
thy will be done
on earth as it is in heaven.
Give us this day our daily bread,
and forgive us our trespasses,
as we forgive those who trespass against us;
and lead us not into temptation,
but deliver us from evil.

BLESSING AND DISMISSAL

Then the celebrant blesses the mothers, holding their children in their
arms, the fathers, and all those present, saying:
The Lord God Almighty,
through his Son, born of the Virgin Mary,
brings joy to Christian mothers
as the hope of eternal life shines forth upon their children.
May he graciously bless the mothers of these children,
so that, as they now give thanks for the gift of their children,
they may always remain united with them in thanksgiving,
in Christ Jesus our Lord.

All:
Amen.

Celebrant:

May the Lord God Almighty,
the giver of life both in heaven and on earth,
bless the fathers of these children,
so that, together with their wives,
they may, by word and example,
prove to be the first witnesses of the faith to their children,
in Christ Jesus our Lord.

All:

Amen.

Celebrant:

May the Lord God Almighty,
who by water and the Holy Spirit
has given us new birth into eternal life,
abundantly bless his faithful here present,
that always and everywhere they may be active members of his people;
and may he bestow his peace on all who are here,
in Christ Jesus our Lord.

All:

Amen.

Celebrant:

May almighty God bless you,
the Father, and the Son, ✠ and the Holy Spirit.

All:

Amen.

Celebrant:

Go in peace.

All:

Thanks be to God.

Other optional formulas of blessing may be used.

After the blessing, if circumstances suggest, a suitable canticle that expresses paschal joy and thanksgiving or the Canticle of the Blessed Virgin Mary, the Magnificat, may be sung by all.

Where it is the custom to bring the baptized infants to the altar of the Blessed Virgin Mary, this custom should appropriately be retained.

ORDER OF BAPTISM FOR ONE CHILD

Rite of Receiving the Child

Baptism should be celebrated, insofar as possible, on a Sunday, the day on which the Church recalls the Paschal Mystery, with the attendance of a large number of the faithful, or at least of the relatives, friends, and neighbors, and with their active participation.

It is for the father and mother, together with the godparents, to present the child to the Church for Baptism.

The faithful sing a suitable Psalm or hymn, if circumstances allow. Meanwhile, the Priest or Deacon celebrant, wearing an alb or surplice and stole, and even a cope, in a festive color, goes with the ministers to the door of the church, or to that part of the church where the parents and godparents are gathered with the child.

The celebrant greets those present, especially the parents and godparents, recalling in a few words the joy with which the parents received their child as a gift from God, who is the source of all life and who now wishes to bestow his own life on him (her). He may use these or similar words:

Dear parents and godparents:
Your family has experienced great joy at the birth of your child,
and the Church shares your happiness.
Today this joy has brought you to the Church
to give thanks to God for the gift of your child
and to celebrate a new birth in the waters of Baptism.
This community rejoices with you,
for today the number of those baptized in Christ will be increased,
and we offer you our support in raising your child
in the practice of the faith.
Therefore, brothers and sisters,
let us now prepare ourselves to participate in this celebration,
listening to God's Word, praying for this child and his (her) family,
and renewing our commitment to the Lord and to his people.

The celebrant first asks the parents of the child:
What name do you give (or: have you given) your child?

Parents:
N.

Celebrant:
What do you ask of God's Church for N.?

Parents:
Baptism.

The celebrant may use other words in this dialogue.

The first reply may be given by another person if, according to local custom, this person has the right to give the name.

In the second reply, the parents may use other words: e.g., Faith or The grace of Christ or Entry into the Church or Eternal life.

Then the celebrant addresses the parents in these or similar words:
In asking for Baptism for your child,
you are undertaking the responsibility
of raising him (her) in the faith,
so that, keeping God's commandments,
he (she) may love the Lord and his (her) neighbor as Christ has
    taught us.
Do you understand this responsibility?

Parents:
We do.

Then turning to the godparents, the celebrant asks in these or similar words:
Are you ready to help the parents of this child in their duty?

Godparents:
We are (I am).

Then the celebrant continues, saying:
N., the Church of God receives you with great joy.
In her name I sign you with the Sign of the Cross of Christ our Savior;
then, after me, your parents (and godparents) will do the same.

And, without saying anything, he signs the child on the forehead.
Afterwards he invites the parents, and if it seems appropriate, the
godparents, to do the same.

The celebrant invites the parents, godparents, and others present to take
part in the celebration of the Word of God. If circumstances permit, a
procession to the appointed place takes place with singing (e.g., Psalm
85 [84]:7-9ab).

PSALM 85 (84):7-9AB

Will you not restore again our life,
that your people may rejoice in you?
Show us, O LORD, your mercy,
and grant us your salvation.
I will hear what the LORD God speaks;
he speaks of peace for his people and his faithful.

Sacred Celebration of the Word of God

BIBLICAL READINGS AND HOMILY

If it seems appropriate, one, or even two, of the following passages is
read, while all are seated.

Mt 28:18-20: *Go, therefore, and make disciples of all nations, baptizing them in
the name of the Father, and of the Son, and of the Holy Spirit* (p. 50).

Mk 1:9-11: *Jesus was baptized in the Jordan by John* (p. 50).

27

Mk 10:13-16: *Let the children come to me; do not prevent them* (p. 51).

Jn 3:1-6: *No one can see the Kingdom of God without being born from above* (p. 52).

The passages that are to be found on pp. 41–46 and 50–56, or others suited to the wishes or needs of the parents, may also be chosen.

Between the Readings, the Responsorial Psalms or the Verses provided on pp. 46–49 may be sung.

After the Reading, the celebrant preaches a brief homily in which light is shed on what has been read, and those present are led to a deeper understanding of the mystery of Baptism and to a more eager fulfillment of the responsibility that arises from it, especially for parents and godparents.

After the Homily, or after the Litany, or even during the Litany, it is recommended that there be a period of silence in which all, invited by the celebrant, pray in their hearts. There follows, if the situation warrants, a suitable liturgical song.

Prayer of the Faithful

Then the Prayer of the Faithful takes place.

Celebrant:
Dear brothers and sisters,
let us invoke the mercy of our Lord Jesus Christ
for this child about to receive the grace of Baptism,
and for his (her) parents, godparents, and all the baptized.

Lector:
Give this child new birth in Baptism
through the radiant divine mystery of your Death and Resurrection,
and join him (her) to your holy Church:

All:
Lord, we ask you, hear our prayer.

Lector:
Make him (her) a faithful disciple and witness to your Gospel
through Baptism and Confirmation:

Lord, we ask you, hear our prayer.

Lead him (her) through holiness of life
to the joys of the heavenly Kingdom:

All:
Lord, we ask you, hear our prayer.

Lector:
Make his (her) parents and godparents
a shining example of the faith to this child:

All:
Lord, we ask you, hear our prayer.

Lector:
Keep his (her) family always in your love:

All:
Lord, we ask you, hear our prayer.

Lector:
Renew the grace of Baptism in each of us:

All:
Lord, we ask you, hear our prayer.

Other optional formulas may be used.

Afterwards, the celebrant invites those present to invoke the aid of the Saints:

Holy Mary, Mother of God,	**pray for us.**
Saint John the Baptist,	**pray for us.**
Saint Joseph,	**pray for us.**
Saint Peter and Saint Paul,	**pray for us.**

It is good to add the names of other Saints, especially the Patron Saint of the child or of the church or of the place. Then the Litany concludes:

All holy men and women, Saints of God,	**pray for us.**

Optional extended form of the Litany may be used.

PRAYER OF EXORCISM AND ANOINTING BEFORE BAPTISM

After the invocations, the celebrant says:

Almighty ever-living God,
who sent your Son into the world
to drive out from us the power of Satan, the spirit of evil,
and bring the human race, rescued from darkness,
into the marvelous Kingdom of your light:
we humbly beseech you
to free this child from Original Sin,
to make him (her) the temple of your glory,
and to grant that your Holy Spirit may dwell in him (her).
Through Christ our Lord.

All:

Amen.

Another formula for the Prayer of Exorcism may be used.

The celebrant continues:

May the strength of Christ the Savior protect you.
As a sign of this we anoint you with the oil of salvation
in the same Christ our Lord,
who lives and reigns for ever and ever.

All:

Amen.

The celebrant anoints the child on the breast with the Oil of
Catechumens.

In the United States, if, for serious reasons, the celebrant judges it
pastorally necessary or desirable, the Anointing before Baptism may be
omitted. In that case, the celebrant says:

May the strength of Christ the Savior protect you;
who lives and reigns for ever and ever.

All:

Amen.

And immediately, without saying anything, he lays his hand on the child.

Then they proceed to the baptistery, or, if circumstances suggest, to the
sanctuary, if the Baptism is celebrated there.

Celebration of Baptism

When they have come to the font, the celebrant briefly reminds those present of the wonderful plan of God, who willed to sanctify the human soul and body through water. He may do this in these or similar words:

A Let us pray, dear brothers and sisters,
that the Lord God Almighty may bestow new life on this child
by water and the Holy Spirit.

Or:

B Dear brothers and sisters,
you know that God graciously bestows
his abundant life through the sacrament of water
on those who believe.
Let us then raise our minds to him,
and with one heart pray
that he may be pleased to pour out his grace from this font
upon this chosen one.

BLESSING OF WATER AND INVOCATION OF GOD OVER THE WATER

Then, turning to the font, the celebrant says the following Blessing (outside Easter Time):

O God, who by invisible power
accomplish a wondrous effect
through sacramental signs
and who in many ways have prepared water, your creation,
to show forth the grace of Baptism;

O God, whose Spirit
in the first moments of the world's creation
hovered over the waters,
so that the very substance of water
would even then take to itself the power to sanctify;

O God, who by the outpouring of the flood
foreshadowed regeneration,
so that from the mystery of one and the same element of water
would come an end to vice and a beginning of virtue;

31

O God, who caused the children of Abraham
to pass dry-shod through the Red Sea,
so that the chosen people,
set free from slavery to Pharaoh,
would prefigure the people of the baptized;

O God, whose Son,
baptized by John in the waters of the Jordan,
was anointed with the Holy Spirit,
and, as he hung upon the Cross,
gave forth water from his side along with blood,
and after his Resurrection, commanded his disciples:
"Go forth, teach all nations, baptizing them
in the name of the Father and of the Son and of the Holy Spirit,"
look now, we pray, upon the face of your Church
and graciously unseal for her the fountain of Baptism.

May this water receive by the Holy Spirit
the grace of your Only Begotten Son,
so that human nature, created in your image
and washed clean through the Sacrament of Baptism
from all the squalor of the life of old,
may be found worthy to rise to the life of newborn children
through water and the Holy Spirit.

The celebrant touches the water with his right hand and continues:
May the power of the Holy Spirit,
O Lord, we pray,
come down through your Son
into the fullness of this font,
so that all who have been buried with Christ
by Baptism into death
may rise again to life with him.
Who lives and reigns for ever and ever.

All:
Amen.

Other optional formulas may be used.

During Easter Time, however, if the baptismal water has been consecrated at the Easter Vigil, so that the Baptism may not lack the element of thanksgiving and petition, the blessing and invocation of God over the water takes place in accordance with the formulas found in the *Order of Baptism*, using the textual variation given at the end of these same formulas.

Renunciation of Sin and Profession of Faith

The celebrant instructs the parents and godparents in these words:

Dear parents and godparents:
through the Sacrament of Baptism
the child you have presented
is about to receive from the love of God
new life by water and the Holy Spirit.

For your part, you must strive to bring him (her) up in the faith, so that this divine life may be preserved from the contagion of sin, and may grow in him (her) day by day.

If your faith makes you ready to accept this responsibility, then, mindful of your own Baptism, renounce sin and profess faith in Christ Jesus, the faith of the Church, in which children are baptized.

Then the celebrant questions the parents and godparents:

A Do you renounce Satan?

Parents and godparents:
I do.

Celebrant:
And all his works?

Parents and godparents:
I do.

Celebrant:
And all his empty show?

Parents and godparents:
I do.

Or:

33

B　Celebrant:

Do you renounce sin,
so as to live in the freedom of the children of God?

Parents and godparents:
I do.

Celebrant:

Do you renounce the lure of evil,
so that sin may have no mastery over you?

Parents and godparents:
I do.

Celebrant:

Do you renounce Satan,
the author and prince of sin?

Parents and godparents:
I do.

In the United States, if the occasion requires, this second formula may
be adapted with more precision by the Diocesan Bishop, especially
when it is necessary that the parents and godparents should renounce
superstitions, divinations, and magical arts practiced with reference to
the child.

Next, the celebrant elicits the threefold profession of faith by the parents
and godparents, saying:

Do you believe in God,
the Father almighty,
Creator of heaven and earth?

Parents and godparents:
I do.

Celebrant:

Do you believe in Jesus Christ, his only Son, our Lord,
who was born of the Virgin Mary,
suffered death and was buried,
rose again from the dead
and is seated at the right hand of the Father?

Parents and godparents:
I do.

Do you believe in the Holy Spirit,
the holy catholic Church,
the communion of saints,
the forgiveness of sins,
the resurrection of the body,
and life everlasting?

Parents and godparents:
I do.

The celebrant, together with the community, gives assent to this
profession of faith, saying:
This is our faith. This is the faith of the Church.
We are proud to profess it in Christ Jesus our Lord.

All:
Amen.

Another formula may be substituted, if circumstances suggest. Or a
suitable liturgical song, by which the community expresses its faith with
one voice, may be sung.

BAPTISM

The celebrant invites the family to approach the font. In addition, using
the name of the child, he asks the parents and godparents:
Is it your will, therefore, that N. should receive Baptism in the faith
of the Church, which we have all professed with you?

Parents and godparents:
It is.

And immediately the celebrant baptizes the child, saying:
N., I BAPTIZE YOU IN THE NAME OF THE FATHER,

He immerses the child or pours water over him (her) a first time.
AND OF THE SON,

He immerses the child or pours water over him (her) a second time.
AND OF THE HOLY SPIRIT.

He immerses the child or pours water over him (her) a third time.

Blessed be God, who chose you in Christ.

Other optional acclamations may be used.

If the Baptism is celebrated by the pouring of water, it is preferable for the child to be held by the mother (or by the father); however, where it is felt that the existing custom should be retained, the child may be held by the godmother (or by the godfather). If the Baptism is by immersion, the child is lifted from the sacred font by the same person.

Explanatory Rites

Anointing after Baptism

Then the celebrant says:

Almighty God, the Father of our Lord Jesus Christ,
has freed you from sin,
given you new birth by water and the Holy Spirit,
and joined you to his people.
He now anoints you with the Chrism of salvation,
so that you may remain as a member of Christ, Priest, Prophet and King,
unto eternal life.

All:

Amen.

Then, without saying anything, the celebrant anoints the child with sacred Chrism on the crown of his (her) head.

Clothing with a White Garment

The celebrant says:

N., you have become a new creation
and have clothed yourself in Christ.
May this white garment be a sign to you of your Christian dignity.
With your family and friends to help you by word and example,
bring it unstained into eternal life.

All:
Amen.

And a white garment is placed on the child; another color is not permitted, unless it is demanded by local custom. It is desirable that the family itself provide this garment.

HANDING ON OF A LIGHTED CANDLE

The celebrant then takes the paschal candle and says:

Receive the light of Christ.

One member of the family (e.g., the father or godfather) lights a candle for the child from the paschal candle.

Then the celebrant says:

Parents and godparents,
this light is entrusted to you to be kept burning brightly,
so that your child, enlightened by Christ,
may walk always as a child of the light
and, persevering in the faith,
may run to meet the Lord when he comes
with all the Saints in the heavenly court.

"EPHPHATHA"

In the United States, the "Ephphatha" Rite takes place at the discretion of the celebrant. The celebrant touches the ears and mouth of the child with his thumb, saying:

May the Lord Jesus,
who made the deaf to hear and the mute to speak,
grant that you may soon receive his word with your ears
and profess the faith with your lips,
to the glory and praise of God the Father.

All:
Amen.

Conclusion of the Rite

Afterwards, unless the Baptism took place in the sanctuary, there is a procession to the altar, in which the lighted candle of the newly baptized child is carried.

Meanwhile, it is desirable that a baptismal canticle be sung, e.g.:
Baptized in Christ,
you are clothed with Christ,
alleluia, alleluia.

Lord's Prayer

The celebrant, standing before the altar, addresses the parents and godparents and all present in these or similar words:
Dear brothers and sisters:
this child, reborn through Baptism,
is now called a child of God, for so indeed he (she) is.

Through Confirmation he (she) will receive the fullness of the Holy Spirit and, approaching the altar of the Lord,
he (she) will share at the table of his Sacrifice,
and will call upon God as Father in the midst of the Church.
Now in his (her) name,
and in the spirit of adoption as sons and daughters
which we all received,
let us pray together as the Lord taught us.

And all say together with the celebrant:
Our Father, who art in heaven,
hallowed be thy name;
thy kingdom come,
thy will be done
on earth as it is in heaven.
Give us this day our daily bread,
and forgive us our trespasses,
as we forgive those who trespass against us;
and lead us not into temptation,
but deliver us from evil.

Blessing and Dismissal

Then the celebrant blesses the mother, holding her child in her arms, the father, and all those present, saying:

The Lord God Almighty,
through his Son, born of the Virgin Mary,
brings joy to Christian mothers
as the hope of eternal life shines forth upon their children.
May he graciously bless the mother of this child,
so that, as she now gives thanks for the gift of her child,
she may always remain united with him (her) in thanksgiving,
in Christ Jesus our Lord.

All:

Amen.

Celebrant:

May the Lord God Almighty,
the giver of life both in heaven and on earth,
bless the father of this child,
so that, together with his wife,
they may, by word and example,
prove to be the first witnesses of the faith to their child,
in Christ Jesus our Lord.

All:

Amen.

Celebrant:

May the Lord God Almighty,
who by water and the Holy Spirit
has given us new birth into eternal life,
abundantly bless his faithful here present,
that always and everywhere they may be active members of his people;
and may he bestow his peace on all who are here,
in Christ Jesus our Lord.

All:

Amen.

May almighty God bless you,
the Father, and the Son, ✟ and the Holy Spirit.

All:

Amen.

Celebrant:

Go in peace.

All:

Thanks be to God.

Other optional formulas of blessing may be used.

After the blessing, if circumstances suggest, a suitable canticle that expresses paschal joy and thanksgiving or the Canticle of the Blessed Virgin Mary, the Magnificat, may be sung by all.

Where it is the custom to bring the baptized infant to the altar of the Blessed Virgin Mary, this custom should appropriately be retained.

BIBLICAL READINGS

(*Lectionary for Mass*, nos. 756–760)

Readings from the Old Testament

1   Ex 17:3-7: *Give us water to drink* (Ex 17:2).

A reading from the Book of Exodus

In their thirst for water,
　　the people grumbled against Moses,
　　saying, "Why did you ever make us leave Egypt?
Was it just to have us die here of thirst
　　with our children and our livestock?"
So Moses cried out to the LORD,
　　"What shall I do with this people?
A little more and they will stone me!"
The LORD answered Moses,
　　"Go over there in front of the people,
　　along with some of the elders of Israel,
　　holding in your hand, as you go,
　　the staff with which you struck the river.
I will be standing there in front of you on the rock in Horeb.
Strike the rock, and the water will flow from it
　　for the people to drink."
This Moses did, in the presence of the elders of Israel.
The place was called Massah and Meribah,
　　because the children of Israel quarreled there
　　and tested the LORD, saying,
　　"Is the LORD in our midst or not?"

The word of the Lord.

2   Ez 36:24-28: *I shall pour clean water upon you to cleanse you from all your impurities.*

A reading from the Book of the Prophet Ezekiel

Thus says the Lord GOD:
I will take you away from among the nations,
    gather you from all the foreign lands,
    and bring you back to your own land.
I will sprinkle clean water upon you
    to cleanse you from all your impurities,
    and from all your idols I will cleanse you.
I will give you a new heart and place a new spirit within you,
    taking from your bodies your stony hearts
    and giving you natural hearts.
I will put my spirit within you and make you live by my statutes,
    careful to observe my decrees.
You shall live in the land I gave your father;
    you shall be my people, and I will be your God.

The word of the Lord.

3   Ez 47:1-9, 12: *I saw water flowing from the temple, and all who were touched by it were saved* (see *Roman Missal*, antiphon for blessing and sprinkling holy water during Easter Time).

A reading from the Book of the Prophet Ezekiel

The angel brought me, Ezekiel,
    back to the entrance of the temple of the Lord,
    and I saw water flowing out
    from beneath the threshold of the temple toward the east,
    for the façade of the temple was toward the east;
    the water flowed down from the right side of the temple,
    south of the altar.
He led me outside by the north gate,
    and around to the outer gate facing the east,
    where I saw water trickling from the right side.
Then when he had walked off to the east
    with a measuring cord in his hand,

he measured off a thousand cubits
and had me wade through the water,
which was ankle-deep.
He measured off another thousand
and once more had me wade through the water,
which was now knee-deep.
Again he measured off a thousand and had me wade;
the water was up to my waist.
Once more he measured off a thousand,
but there was now a river through which I could not wade;
for the water had risen so high it had become a river
that could not be crossed except by swimming.
He asked me, "Have you seen this, son of man?"
Then he brought me to the bank of the river, where he had me sit.
Along the bank of the river I saw very many trees on both sides.
He said to me,
"This water flows into the eastern district down upon the Arabah,
and empties into the sea, the salt waters, which it makes fresh.
Wherever the river flows,
every sort of living creature that can multiply shall live,
and there shall be abundant fish,
for wherever this water comes the sea shall be made fresh.
Along both banks of the river, fruit trees of every kind shall grow;
their leaves shall not fade, nor their fruit fail.
Every month they shall bear fresh fruit,
for they shall be watered by the flow from the sanctuary.
Their fruit shall serve for food, and their leaves for medicine."

The word of the Lord.

Readings from the New Testament

1 Rom 6:3-5: *Buried with him through baptism into death, we too might live in newness of life.*

A reading from the Letter of Saint Paul to the Romans

Brothers and sisters:
Are you unaware that we who were baptized into Christ Jesus
    were baptized into his death?
We were indeed buried with him through baptism into death,
    so that, just as Christ was raised from the dead
    by the glory of the Father,
    we too might live in newness of life.

For if we have grown into union with him through a death like his,
    we shall also be united with him in the resurrection.

The word of the Lord.

2 Rom 8:28-32: *To be conformed to the image of his Son.*

A reading from the Letter of Saint Paul to the Romans

Brothers and sisters:
We know that all things work for good for those who love God,
    who are called according to his purpose.
For those he foreknew he also predestined
    to be conformed to the image of his Son,
    so that he might be the firstborn
    among many brothers.
And those he predestined he also called;
    and those he called he also justified;
    and those he justified he also glorified.
What then shall we say to this?
If God is for us, who can be against us?
He who did not spare his own Son
    but handed him over for us all,
    how will he not also give us everything else along with him?

The word of the Lord.

3   1 Cor 12:12-13: *For in one Spirit we were all baptized into one Body.*

A reading from the first Letter of Saint Paul to the Corinthians

Brothers and sisters:
As a body is one though it has many parts,
    and all the parts of the body, though many, are one body,
    so also Christ.
For in one Spirit we were all baptized into one Body,
    whether Jews or Greeks, slaves or free persons,
    and we were all given to drink of one Spirit.

The word of the Lord.

4   Gal 3:26-28: *All of you who were baptized into Christ have clothed yourselves with Christ.*

A reading from the Letter of Saint Paul to the Galatians

Brothers and sisters:
Through faith you are all children of God in Christ Jesus.
For all of you who were baptized into Christ
    have clothed yourselves with Christ.
There is neither Jew nor Greek,
    there is neither slave nor free person,
    there is not male and female;
    for you are all one in Christ Jesus.

The word of the Lord.

5   Eph 4:1-6: *There is one Lord, one faith, one baptism.*

A reading from the Letter of Saint Paul to the Ephesians

Brothers and sisters:
I, a prisoner for the Lord,
    urge you to live in a manner worthy of the call you have received,
    with all humility and gentleness, with patience,
    bearing with one another through love,
    striving to preserve the unity of the spirit
    through the bond of peace:

45

one Body and one Spirit,
as you were also called to the one hope of your call;
one Lord, one faith, one baptism;
one God and Father of all,
who is over all and through all and in all.

The word of the Lord.

6   1 Pt 2:4-5, 9-10: *You are a chosen race, a royal priesthood.*

A reading from the first Letter of Saint Peter

Beloved:
Come to the Lord, a living stone, rejected by human beings
    but chosen and precious in the sight of God,
    and, like living stones,
    let yourselves be built into a spiritual house
    to be a holy priesthood to offer spiritual sacrifices
        acceptable to God through Jesus Christ.
You are "a chosen race, a royal priesthood,
    a holy nation, a people of his own,
    so that you may announce the praises" of him
    who called you out of darkness into his wonderful light.

    Once you were "no people"
        but now you are God's people;
    you "had not received mercy"
        but now you have received mercy.

The word of the Lord.

Responsorial Psalms

1   Ps 23 (22):1-3a, 3b-4, 5, 6

℟. (1) **The Lord is my shepherd; there is nothing I shall want.**

The LORD is my shepherd;
    there is nothing I shall want.

Fresh and green are the pastures
  where he gives me repose.
Near restful waters he leads me;
  he revives my soul. R℘.

He guides me along the right path,
  for the sake of his name.
Though I should walk in the valley of the shadow of death,
  no evil would I fear, for you are with me.
Your crook and your staff will give me comfort. R℘.

You have prepared a table before me
  in the sight of my foes.
My head you have anointed with oil;
  my cup is overflowing. R℘.

Surely goodness and mercy shall follow me
  all the days of my life.
In the LORD's own house shall I dwell
  for length of days unending. R℘.

2   Ps 27 (26):1, 4, 8b-9abcd, 13-14

R℘. (1a) **The Lord is my light and my salvation.**
  or:
R℘. (Eph 5:14) **Wake up and rise from death: Christ will shine
  upon you!**

The LORD is my light and my salvation;
  whom shall I fear?
The LORD is the stronghold of my life;
  whom should I dread? R℘.

There is one thing I ask of the LORD,
  only this do I seek:
to live in the house of the LORD
  all the days of my life,
to gaze on the beauty of the LORD,
  to inquire at his temple. R℘.

It is your face, O Lord, that I seek;
    hide not your face from me.
Dismiss not your servant in anger;
    you have been my help.
Do not abandon me. R⁄.

I believe I shall see the Lord's goodness
    in the land of the living.
Wait for the Lord; be strong;
    be stouthearted, and wait for the Lord! R⁄.

3   Ps 34 (33):2-3, 6-7, 8-9, 14-15, 16-17, 18-19

R⁄. (6a) **Look to him, that you may be radiant with joy!**
    or:
R⁄. (9a) **Taste and see the goodness of the Lord.**

I will bless the Lord at all times;
    praise of him is always in my mouth.
In the Lord my soul shall make its boast;
    the humble shall hear and be glad. R⁄.

Look toward him and be radiant;
    let your faces not be abashed.
This lowly one called; the Lord heard,
    and rescued him from all his distress. R⁄.

The angel of the Lord is encamped
    around those who fear him, to rescue them.
Taste and see that the Lord is good.
    Blessed the man who seeks refuge in him. R⁄.

Guard your tongue from evil,
    and your lips from speaking deceit.
Turn aside from evil and do good.
    Seek after peace, and pursue it. R⁄.

The Lord turns his eyes to the just one,
    and his ears are open to his cry.
The Lord turns his face against the wicked
    to cut off their remembrance from the earth. R⁄.

When the just one cries out, the LORD hears,
 and rescues him in all his distress.
The LORD is close to the brokenhearted;
 those whose spirit is crushed he will save. ℟.

Alleluia Verse and Verse before the Gospel

1 Jn 3:16

God so loved the world that he gave his only-begotten Son,
so that everyone who believes in him might have eternal life.

2 Jn 8:12

I am the light of the world, says the Lord;
whoever follows me will have the light of life.

3 Jn 14:6

I am the way and the truth and the life, says the Lord;
no one comes to the Father, except through me.

4 Eph 4:5-6

There is one Lord, one faith, one baptism,
one God and the Father of all.

5 Cf. 2 Tm 1:10

Our Savior Jesus Christ has destroyed death
and brought life to light through the Gospel.

6 1 Pt 2:9

You are a chosen race, a royal priesthood, a holy nation:
announce the praises of him who called you
out of darkness into his wonderful light.

Gospel

1   Mt 22:35-40: *This is the greatest and the first commandment.*

✛ A reading from the holy Gospel according to Matthew

One of the Pharisees, a scholar of the law, tested Jesus by asking,
   "Teacher, which commandment in the law is the greatest?"
He said to him,
   "You shall love the Lord, your God, with all your heart,
   with all your soul, and with all your mind.
This is the greatest and the first commandment.
The second is like it:
   You shall love your neighbor as yourself.
The whole law and the prophets depend on these two commandments."

The Gospel of the Lord.

2   Mt 28:18-20: *Go, therefore, and make disciples of all nations, baptizing them in the name of the Father, and of the Son, and of the Holy Spirit.*

✛ A reading from the holy Gospel according to Matthew

Jesus said to the Eleven disciples,
"All power in heaven and on earth has been given to me.
Go, therefore, and make disciples of all nations,
   baptizing them in the name of the Father,
   and of the Son, and of the Holy Spirit,
   teaching them to observe all that I have commanded you.
And behold, I am with you always, until the end of the age.

The Gospel of the Lord.

3   Mk 1:9-11: *Jesus was baptized in the Jordan by John.*

✛ A reading from the holy Gospel according to Mark

Jesus came from Nazareth of Galilee
   and was baptized in the Jordan by John.
On coming up out of the water he saw the heavens being torn open
   and the Spirit, like a dove, descending upon him.

And a voice came from the heavens,
"You are my beloved Son; with you I am well pleased."

The Gospel of the Lord.

4   Mk 10:13-16: *Let the children come to me; do not prevent them.*

✠ A reading from the holy Gospel according to Mark

People were bringing children to Jesus that he might touch them,
but the disciples rebuked them.
When Jesus saw this he became indignant and said to them,
"Let the children come to me; do not prevent them,
for the Kingdom of God belongs to such as these.
Amen, I say to you,
whoever does not accept the Kingdom of God like a child
will not enter it."
Then he embraced them and blessed them,
placing his hands on them.

The Gospel of the Lord.

5   Long Form   Mk 12:28b-34: *Hear O Israel! You shall love the Lord, your God,*
                        with all your heart.

✠ A reading from the holy Gospel according to Mark

One of the scribes came to Jesus and asked him,
"Which is the first of all the commandments?"
Jesus replied, "The first is this:
Hear, O Israel!
The Lord our God is Lord alone!
You shall love the Lord your God with all your heart,
with all your soul, with all your mind,
and with all your strength.
The second is this:
You shall love your neighbor as yourself.
There is no other commandment greater than these."
The scribe said to him,
"Well said, teacher. You are right in saying,
'He is One and there is no other than he.'

51

And 'to love him with all your heart,
  with all your understanding,
  with all your strength,
  and to love your neighbor as yourself'
  is worth more than all burnt offerings and sacrifices."
And when Jesus saw that he answered with understanding,
  he said to him,
  "You are not far from the Kingdom of God."
And no one dared to ask him any more questions.

The Gospel of the Lord.

or Short Form   Mk 12:28b-31: *Hear O Israel! You shall love the Lord, your God, with all your heart.*

✛ A reading from the holy Gospel according to Mark

One of the scribes came to Jesus and asked him,
  "Which is the first of all the commandments?"
Jesus replied, "The first is this:
  Hear, O Israel!
  The Lord our God is Lord alone!
You shall love the Lord your God with all your heart,
  with all your soul, with all your mind,
  and with all your strength.
The second is this:
  You shall love your neighbor as yourself.
There is no other commandment greater than these."

The Gospel of the Lord.

6   Jn 3:1-6: *No one can see the Kingdom of God without being born from above.*

✛ A reading from the holy Gospel according to John

There was a Pharisee named Nicodemus, a ruler of the Jews.
He came to Jesus at night and said to him,
  "Rabbi, we know that you are a teacher who has come from God,
  for no one can do these signs that you are doing
  unless God is with him."
Jesus answered and said to him,

"Amen, amen, I say to you,
  unless one is born from above,
  he cannot see the Kingdom of God."
Nicodemus said to him,
  "How can a man once grown old be born again?
Surely he cannot reenter his mother's womb and be born again, can he?"
Jesus answered,
  "Amen, amen, I say to you,
  unless one is born of water and Spirit
  he cannot enter the Kingdom of God.
What is born of flesh is flesh
  and what is born of spirit is spirit."

The Gospel of the Lord.

7   Jn 4:5-14: *A spring of water welling up to eternal life.*

✝ A reading from the holy Gospel according to John

Jesus came to a town of Samaria called Sychar,
  near the plot of land that Jacob had given to his son Joseph.
Jacob's well was there.
Jesus, tired from his journey, sat down there at the well.
It was about noon.

A woman of Samaria came to draw water.
Jesus said to her,
  "Give me a drink."
His disciples had gone into the town to buy food.
The Samaritan woman said to him,
  "How can you, a Jew, ask me, a Samaritan woman, for a drink?"
—For Jews use nothing in common with Samaritans.—
Jesus answered and said to her,
  "If you knew the gift of God
  and who is saying to you, 'Give me a drink,'
  you would have asked him
  and he would have given you living water."
The woman said to him,
  "Sir, you do not even have a bucket and the cistern is deep;
  where then can you get this living water?

53

Are you greater than our father Jacob,
  who gave us this cistern and drank from it himself
  with his children and his flocks?"
Jesus answered and said to her,
  "Everyone who drinks this water will be thirsty again;
  but whoever drinks the water I shall give will never thirst;
  the water I shall give will become in him
  a spring of water welling up to eternal life."

The Gospel of the Lord.

8   Jn 6:44-47: *Whoever believes has eternal life.*

✣ A reading from the holy Gospel according to John

Jesus said to the crowds:
"No one can come to me unless the Father who sent me draw him,
  and I will raise him on the last day.
It is written in the prophets:
  They shall all be taught by God.
Everyone who listens to my Father and learns from him comes to me.
Not that anyone has seen the Father
  except the one who is from God;
  he has seen the Father.
Amen, amen, I say to you,
  whoever believes has eternal life."

The Gospel of the Lord.

9   Jn 7:37b-39a: *Rivers of living water will flow.*

✣ A reading from the holy Gospel according to John

Jesus stood up and exclaimed,
  "Let anyone who thirsts come to me and drink.
Whoever believes in me, as Scripture says:
  Rivers of living water will flow from within him."
He said this in reference to the Spirit
  that those who came to believe in him were to receive.

The Gospel of the Lord.

✠ A reading from the holy Gospel according to John

As Jesus passed by he saw a man blind from birth.
His disciples asked him,
    "Rabbi, who sinned, this man or his parents,
    that he was born blind?"
Jesus answered,
    "Neither he nor his parents sinned;
    it is so that the works of God might be made visible through him.
We have to do the works of the one who sent me while it is day.
Night is coming when no one can work.
While I am in the world, I am the light of the world."
When he had said this, he spat on the ground
    and made clay with the saliva,
    and smeared the clay on his eyes, and said to him,
    "Go wash in the Pool of Siloam" (which means Sent).
So he went and washed, and came back able to see.

The Gospel of the Lord.

11   Jn 15:1-11: *Whoever remains in me and I in him will bear much fruit.*

✠ A reading from the holy Gospel according to John

Jesus said to his disciples:
"I am the true vine, and my Father is the vine grower.
He takes away every branch in me that does not bear fruit,
    and everyone that does he prunes so that it bears more fruit.
You are already pruned because of the word that I spoke to you.
Remain in me, as I remain in you.
Just as a branch cannot bear fruit on its own
    unless it remains on the vine,
    so neither can you unless you remain in me.
I am the vine, you are the branches.
Whoever remains in me and I in him will bear much fruit,
    because without me you can do nothing.
Anyone who does not remain in me
    will be thrown out like a branch and wither;

people will gather them and throw them into a fire
and they will be burned.
If you remain in me and my words remain in you,
ask for whatever you want and it will be done for you.
By this is my Father glorified,
that you bear much fruit and become my disciples.
As the Father loves me, so I also love you.
Remain in my love.
If you keep my commandments, you will remain in my love,
just as I have kept my Father's commandments
and remain in his love.

"I have told you this so that my joy may be in you
and your joy may be complete."

The Gospel of the Lord.

---

12   Jn 19:31-35: *One soldier thrust his lance into his side, and immediately Blood and water flowed out.*

✣ A reading from the holy Gospel according to John

Since it was preparation day,
in order that the bodies might not remain on the cross on the
sabbath,
for the sabbath day of that week was a solemn one,
the Jews asked Pilate that their legs be broken
and they be taken down.
So the soldiers came and broke the legs of the first
and then of the other one who was crucified with Jesus.
But when they came to Jesus and saw that he was already dead,
they did not break his legs,
but one soldier thrust his lance into his side,
and immediately Blood and water flowed out.
An eyewitness has testified, and his testimony is true;
he knows that he is speaking the truth,
so that you also may come to believe.

The Gospel of the Lord.